I am Ana

and I am Breaking the Silence

**One Woman's Journey
to Triumph Over
Domestic Violence**

Ana Williams

I am Ana

AMA Legacy, LLC

824 Lake Ave 366, Lake Worth Beach FL 33460-3754

https://amalegacy.org/

ISBN 979-8-9869212-0-4 (paperback)

ISBN 979-8-9869212-1-1 (hardcover)

What People Are Saying

"I am Ana and I am Breaking the Silence is full of power and punch about the story of a woman's survival and victory over domestic violence. Every mother should give her daughter a copy of this book before she begins to date."
-Maureen Ryan Blake, Maureen Ryan Blake Media Production

"Ana shares how a little hope, faith, prayer, courage and support from others changed her life. Ana was once a silent sufferer of domestic violence, to become an author, advocate, and speaker for abusive domestic violence. A must-read as your life or someone you love can also change.
-Toni Stone Bruce, Author, Motivational Speaker, Coach
Founder/CEO Precious Stones 4 Life, LLC

"This book is a powerful tool in the battle against domestic violence."
-MacKenzie Nelson, Best-Selling International Author "My Father's Feathers"

Table of Contents

Dedication

This book is dedicated to my beautiful mother, Mirian, who was my very best friend and worked so hard to raise our family and keep us safe.

Acknowledgments

I am so grateful to be alive today and to be able to tell my story. I want to express my gratitude to those who have helped me through my difficult journey, who love and support me today, and who have encouraged me to bring my experience into the light so that others may be inspired by it to triumph over their own experiences of domestic violence.

I thank God for all He has done to bring me through my journey and give me the courage to tell my story publicly.

I am thankful for my husband, for his patient and unending support through the difficult task of reliving my horrifying experiences over and over so I could set them down on paper for this book. He is a double blessing in my life.

To my beautiful children, who weathered these storms with me for so many years and who inspired me to break the silence, I am deeply grateful and love you always.

I give thanks to the family and friends who supported and protected my children and me in so many ways, large and small, that literally saved my life and gave me the strength to build a new one. I wish I could name you all, but you know who you are and how much I love you. I'm also thankful for the neighbors and strangers who touched my life, maybe for just a few moments, like tiny sparks of light that showed me I was worth more than the suffering I was experiencing.

And my thanks to Bettyanne for helping me find the words of my heart to tell my story so beautifully, and to the RHG Media Productions Team for standing with me all along the way to help me break my silence and share my message out into the world.

Introduction

Nearly 20 people per minute are victims of physical violence by an intimate partner in the United States. During one year, this equates to more than 10 million women and men. (https://www.projectsanctuary.org/dv/some-statistics-about-domestic-violence/)

About 1 in 4 women have experienced sexual violence, physical violence and/or stalking by an intimate partner during their lifetime. (https://www.cdc.gov/violenceprevention/intimatepartnerviolence/fastfact.html)

Over one-half of female homicide victims in the U.S. are killed by a current or former male intimate partner. (https://www.cdc.gov/violenceprevention/intimatepartnerviolence/fastfact.html)

Every day, more than 20,000 phone calls are placed to domestic violence hotlines nationwide. (https://www.thinkmedfirst.com/domestic-violence/)

These statistics are startling and scary. And they don't really represent the reality for each one of those millions of women and their children – who have lived through domestic violence in their own homes and relationships.

In this book, I want to hold a candle to these women – because I am one of them.

I am telling my own story so that people can understand what it is like for these women on a daily basis, over weeks and months and years. I want for people to realize that many more individuals have suffered through the experience of abuse and never reported it – or never made it through alive.

Many people, often meaning well, will ask, *Why don't they just leave their abusers?*

It is not that easy. You loved (and may still love) this person. You have birthed his children, and you feel confused by his behavior, hoping it will change, always looking for that tiny part of him that you fell in love with. Before you know it, you become trapped, ashamed, alone, and afraid.

And you see no way out.

I hope when you read my story, you will understand how and why this can happen to a woman and, happily, how women like me can triumph over domestic violence.

I do not tell my story for the purpose of revenge or to harm anyone, including my abuser. I am telling my story for those women who feel they are alone, trapped, and afraid like I was. I want to help as many women as I can – my granddaughters, your daughters, my neighbors, your neighbors – anybody I come across. I want to touch their hearts. I want to tell them this: ***You are not alone. You are beautiful. You do not deserve to be mistreated. Keep up your faith! There is a way out – and it is worth it!***

In the back of this book, you will find the toll-free number for the National Domestic Violence Hotline. Please share this resource with anyone you believe may need assistance with an experience of domestic violence in any form. I keep this number on my phone and carry it with me always so I can share it with someone who may need it. I also share out this information every time I speak to groups about domestic violence. You never know when you may cross the path of someone who needs support... and life-saving help can be just one call away.

Chapter One

Once Upon a Time

Once upon a time, a little girl lived in a small town in El Salvador with her mother, father, five brothers, and two sisters. She was the middle child in this large family, struggling to make ends meet in an impoverished, war-torn country. Their sole income came from her dad who was a taxi driver; her mom worked hard at home to raise their family and keep them safe.

This little girl was born into the Seventh-day Adventist Church; her upbringing was wholesome, sheltered, and strict. There was no drinking or smoking in the household, and her parents did their best to protect their children from the drugs and violence swirling around them in the barrio. Her dad was stern and kept her inside the house most of the time, but he could always make her laugh, and she knew he loved her and would protect her.

What a lively little girl she was! She loved to sing and dance. She would make up magical events, like a Miss Universe Pageant, where she, of course, was the host. Her grandpa helped her put lights up in the backyard, and her neighbors would be the judges. Her mom, who was her very best friend, called her "the actress." Mom always made sure that her daughter had fun and looked (and felt) beautiful, even in spite of the challenging times.

Although they lived a difficult life in the barrio, they were a happy family. Every Saturday, they loved going to church with their loving community. Christmas may not have included any presents, but there were always family gatherings and good food. She loved to help get the tree and decorate it with lights each year.

Even though her dreams were big, she lived a sheltered life and didn't know much of the world beyond her home. Then everything changed...

When she was 18, her family escaped from the war in their country, and they traveled to America with the hope of opportunity and freedom—only to discover the other side of her dream.

This is her story.

Chapter Two

Life in a Dream World

I was 25 years old, renting a room from my friend Angela and working in a jewelry story downtown. We were poor, but we had fun. My road to this point had been difficult – my very roots had been pulled up to escape to America. I didn't get to graduate from high school in my country, and I spoke no English, teaching myself mainly from watching the news and television shows. I had been so sheltered that I didn't know how to socialize and felt shy with others most of the time, mainly because my poor English felt like a barrier. But I was so grateful to be here; I loved this country and the city I was living in, my family was around me, and I was making my way in this new, exciting world.

Angela loved to go out to clubs, which was not my thing. One night, we went out for dinner. When we finished, Angela wanted me to come with her to the club because she wanted to meet and get to know the bouncer so he would let them into the club for free. I didn't want to go. I just wanted to go home and sleep in. She begged me, *Come on, Ana! Do this for me! We won't stay long, I promise!* I still declined, and she promised to take me home. However, on the way, she stopped by the club, and I felt obligated to get out of the car and go in with her.

We weren't there long when a guy asked Angela to dance. She was dressed very pretty, so she went right out onto the dance floor. I felt self-conscious in my jeans and sweatshirt, so I just stood outside the dance floor, by myself, looking around feeling a little stupid, waiting for her to have fun so we could go back home.

Suddenly, I felt a tap on my shoulder, and I turned around to see a handsome, tall, very muscular man smiling at me. It was the bouncer Angela was wanting to meet! He asked my name and if I wanted a drink. *I don't drink,* I said, *but I'll take a soda. Okay,* he replied, *Don't go away, I'll be right back.*

He turned toward the bar and as he disappeared into the crowd. I watched him, wondering why he would be bothering with me – there were so many beautiful girls around. I caught Angela's eye on the dance floor, and she smiled wide and gave me a thumbs-up sign. Since she'd be so happy if I got to know him, and he could let us in the club for free next time. I thought I'd stay and talk to him if he came back.

Sure enough, he returned in a few minutes with my soda, and we began to talk. His name was John, and he was very charming and kind to me. Throughout the night, he would go back and forth, talking with other people, but always coming back to my side. He seemed popular, and I liked watching the people he was with laughing and enjoying each other. I began to feel proud that he had chosen me to come back to.

At one point toward the end of the evening, John asked for my number and then whispered to me, *You're going to be the mother of my children.* It felt surprising and sweet to hear, but I didn't pay it any mind. Angela and I left the club soon after and even though I was attracted to him, I did not expect to ever see him again.

Well, John called me the next morning. I was self-conscious about my broken English over the phone, but he didn't seem to mind at all. We started to date. He took me to expensive restaurants, and we would go out with his friends, who were nice people.

We'd been dating about two weeks when we went to his friend's pool party. As we approached the long, winding, tree-lined driveway, what suddenly appeared before me was a gorgeous mansion. It was the first time in my life that I had ever seen a real mansion! My eyes must have been as big as saucers as I peered into the huge rooms with their fancy furnishings and through to the outdoors, where there was a sparkling blue swimming pool.

I felt like I was in a magical, wonderful dream as John and I swam together in this magnificent pool among beautiful, elegant, happy people.

As we sat together in the sauna, John told me for the first time that he really cared about me and wanted to have a serious relationship. I was so happy because to me he was like Prince Charming in a fairy tale!

We started seeing a lot of each other and spending hours on the phone. Sometimes he would show up at my door unexpectedly to tell me he missed me. It felt odd to hear him say that, but I was so taken up in this whirlwind romance I chose not to think anything of it. When we were with his friends, he called me his girlfriend. I was thrilled and could hardly believe how lucky I was to be with this man.

We had a lot of fun together, and I was grateful that he did not care about my broken English, or ever made fun of my strong accent. It was sometimes hard to understand each other because I was still learning English, but little by little, I was learning how to communicate better.

He was always checking on me, which I thought was his way of being extra sweet and caring. I had been in a relationship before which had produced my beautiful son Luis. For some time now, I had been alone, working and raising my son. Now, here was someone who helped me feel safe and protected.

Our life together was exciting because he knew a lot of people who lived in amazing places and knew how to throw huge, fun parties. I never drank alcohol or had anything to do with drugs, but I didn't mind the parties as nothing seemed to get out of hand. Just people having fun.

After a few months, I began to see more of his character come out. At first, I thought it was just a natural part of having a relationship – with growing love comes seeing your partner in their low times as well as their best times. But I had this feeling that John was starting to change in ways that I did not understand. His moods would shift dramatically – one moment he was happy and the next moment he was irritated, and the next cracking jokes, so I wasn't sure what was coming next.

It was hard for me to understand what was going on with him, and I began to think that maybe I wasn't being nice enough or fair to him. I thought maybe he was just tired from working nights. So, I gave him the benefit of the doubt – and I tried harder to be the girlfriend he wanted me to be.

One day, I didn't hear from him for a long time, so I called him and he didn't answer the phone, which was unusual. I started to worry about him and called off and on all day. No answer.

The next afternoon, he called me back, and I asked, *What's wrong? Are you okay?* He snapped back, *Nothing's wrong!* Then he went into a long monologue about how he was mad at me because he was ready to start a new life with me and I was not showing much interest. I was surprised – we had just met! I told him, *This is so soon, but if you really think that it can work out, then I guess I can think about it. And what about Luis?*

Luis was three years old and my pride and joy. I knew better than to marry and I was scared to go too fast because I needed to make sure my son would be okay. I was very close to my family who lived nearby. My son and I had been doing fine. But John seemed to like Luis and was generous and kind to him, and my family seemed to like John.

Finally, he convinced me to move in together. I was a little worried about how everything seemed to be going so fast. But I knew that if things didn't work out, I had my family near me and would still have a place for my son and me.

So, we formed a little family and moved in together across the street from my older sister's house. I was overjoyed! I thought I had found my Prince Charming and that this was true love. John was very kind and loving. He would shower me with all kinds of gifts like clothes, shoes, flowers, money. He would be spontaneous and say, *Pack your bags, Ana, in two hours, we're leaving to catch a plane!* We'd fly somewhere out of state, and I would be so excited about traveling. It didn't matter whether I was flying or driving, it was just that I had never dreamed I could have experiences like this in my life, having grown up so impoverished and sheltered.

I was aware that he was trying to impress me with materialistic things. He liked for me to dress up so he could show me off to his friends at parties and different events. I started to dress differently than I had before, and it felt a little uncomfortable – not really my style. But this was all so new to me, and now I looked like his friends and the people in his life. It was another world, and I thought it was exciting.

And... it was another world that was moving so fast I could hardly keep up! I really did not know anything about John. He would mention that his sisters were famous, but I didn't believe him, because I never saw them while we were dating. In fact, I never saw his family at all. And with my problems with English, I didn't understand much of what he was telling me. When he took me out, I was always at his side, looking beautiful (he said), and most of the time, I smiled more than I talked.

We were happy, at least for these first months. I'm not going to lie, I was thrilled to see a whole new life that I had never had, one that was possible for me and for my son. I never cared about having gifts or going to exotic places, all the glitz and the glitter, or celebrity. I was, and still am, a simple person who loves simple things.

But I told myself that here was this incredible man

who would reach the stars and bring one to me. I made up a story in my head about how wonderful and perfect my life would be.

Here was my Prince Charming, and, looking back, I see that I desperately wanted to believe it.

Chapter Three

Where is My Prince Charming?

About three months after we moved in together, I came home from work on a Sunday and thought, *What in the world is happening at my house?* There were cars parked all up and down the street, music and laughter, and the aroma of barbeque coming from our backyard. John came out the front door to greet me and tell me he had a surprise for me.

A party was going on, and all his friends were there having a good time. I walked around to say hello to all of them. I'd barely gotten myself a soda when John raised his arms up and shouted, *Quiet, quiet, everybody! I have something to say!*

John then turned to face me, pulled a tiny box out of his jacket pocket, and said in front of everyone: *Ana, will you marry me?*

I was shocked! None of my family or friends were there, and inside my head, thoughts were racing: *What do I say? I barely know you! Why now? Everybody's here, and I don't want to embarrass you and say no! It's too soon... Do you really love me?*

I believed he loved me. My head and heart were full of emotion. There was all this happy chatter around me, and all eyes were on me. I heard myself say, *Yes*.

The rest of the afternoon was crazy because inside of me, I was shouting, *WHAT DID I DO?*

As I laid my head on the pillow that night, I told myself that he would love me and protect me.

I was so wrong.

———————

Not long after we moved in together, I was already noticing that he would go out to the club by himself, and sometimes come back early the next morning. He would ask me if I wanted to go with him, which I would sometimes do, but often, I had Luis, I was tired from work, or I just didn't want to be with everyone else while they were drinking. I didn't think too much of it because I trusted him – I had learned trust from my parents and that's how I lived my life.

But one day, I passed by his car in the driveway and noticed something lying on the floor – it was his underwear. So, I asked him why it was there. He immediately got upset and shouted, *Why are you searching my car??* I answered, *I am not searching your car. It was just there on the floor.* He glared at me and yelled, *Well, it's nothing – don't worry about it!* I was so surprised that

I just stopped and closed my mouth. I didn't want to say anything that would make the argument get worse.

This was the first time I had ever seen John so upset, watching him about to explode and straining to get control of himself. I stayed silent. In a few moments, he was back to his old self, nice and charming, cracking jokes to diffuse the situation.

I soon let the whole thing go because he seemed to be doing his best to make up for it. I was willing to trust anything.

The first time I met his family, something struck me that I would later think about a lot. As we were sitting in their living room getting to know each other, my mother-in-law, Claudia, said to John: *Be good to Ana. She is the nicest thing that could ever happen in your life.* It seemed like an odd thing to say, but I smiled because I was flattered that she would say something like that and it seemed to show that she genuinely liked me. As we were heading back to the house, he seemed overjoyed that his stepmother had embraced me and my son.

Life went on, coming home from work to impromptu parties with his friends at our house, taking me out and showing me off to new friends, and showering Luis and me with gifts. To me, he was brilliant – his ear-to-ear smile, jokes, kindness and charm. I was too preoccupied and in love to see anything else.

I was totally unaware that I was in the arms of a beast.

———————

About four months later, we moved from across the street from my sister to another location in the city. I was unable to visit my mother as frequently as I had when we lived nearby, especially since I didn't own a car. When I did go to see her, the house phone would ring minutes after I arrived. It would be John.

Is there any reason why your man is calling you so much? my mother would ask me. *He loves me,* I would respond, *and he likes being with me, and he misses me.* My mother would shake her head, *That makes no sense! You just left your house, and he can't possibly miss you that much when you live 20 minutes away.* I began to believe that what my mother was telling me was true.

It became increasingly worse. I noticed that he would call me at my job, and the phone would ring the moment I stepped inside the house from work or shopping. At first, it was sweet to have someone always checking on me, "protecting" me.

One day, my boss took me aside to warn me to be cautious with John, saying he wasn't so sure he was a good fit for me. I said thanks but I didn't listen to him or anyone of my other friends who were beginning to tell me the same thing. I convinced myself that they were just bashing him because they were bigoted.

Then I noticed that he was following me a lot, even showing up at my job. Once, my coworkers invited me to a barbeque over the weekend, and John insisted on coming with me so I would be "safe." I was so naïve that I truly did not understand that it was about him wanting to control me. More of my friends were telling me they didn't like him and to be very careful about him.

But I wouldn't listen – I couldn't listen.

Soon, John decided he would drop me off and pick me up from work, which made me happy because I'd been taking the bus every day, this was going to be much more convenient. But as time went on, I would often smell women's perfume clinging to the passenger side seatbelt I was using. If I asked who else had been in the car, he would snap, *Why are you asking me a stupid question like that?* If I answered that I smelled perfume, he would call me crazy. I knew he was lying about women in his car, but I talked myself into thinking it might be just one of his female friends. And it was easier to stay silent than to make him angry.

It wasn't long before he started picking me up late from work more and more often. One day, he was super late, so I thought something must have come up and I decided to take the bus home on my own. Along the way home,

I happened to casually look out the window and, to my surprise, there was his car driving along next to the bus!

John was following me. He must have been watching me come out of work to have known I was taking the bus (we didn't have cellphones back then to track someone's location). Was he trying to see if I was talking to a man or something more? It was crazy!

When I got off the bus at my stop, his car pulled up in front of it, he called out the open window for me to get in the car, and we drove the rest of the way home. I was silent for a while with sadness washing over me. This didn't make any sense. I was not doing anything to make him feel I was cheating on him or being unfaithful in any way. I could feel that HE was angry, which also made no sense because, of course, he was the one who left me waiting for 45 minutes!

I wanted to say, *How dare you do this to me? I am good to you and I love you. Are you so insecure that you would hide from me to catch me doing something that I would never do?* But I said nothing, thinking there must be a reason – and it must be my fault.

Looking back on it now, I was the perfect target for someone like John. I was so innocent and trusting and ignorant. I came from a different country and culture, and my language was a barrier to really communicating with him and understanding him and for him to understand me (maybe that was exactly the way he liked it). I have no idea why I believed his stories, his lies and excuses, but I did.

I just could not comprehend what was really happening and what kind of person would treat their wife in this way.

———————

John became more and more obsessed with me. He was literally trying to dictate how I was to live my life – who I could hang with, where I could go. I loved being around my friends, so why did I have to stop seeing them? I didn't get it.

John would say, *They're not really your friends. You don't need them. I am your friend. It's simple, you don't need no one around you. I will always be there for you.*

If I tried to argue with him, we got nowhere. I began telling a friend that I couldn't have dinner with her or go to a party or whatever it was, each time making up an excuse because I was too embarrassed to tell the true reason. Then I would go up to my room for another lonely evening, while he was out at the club or with his friends. I was getting sadder and sadder, realizing that I had made a mistake and not sure if I could break up with him.

I loved John, and it was so hard to see it all clearly. I felt uncertain about my future, so I decided to wait a little more, be kind and patient and see if he would change his ways. However, something wasn't quite right – I didn't quite believe what I was trying to tell myself. Something inside of me wanted me to pay attention, and I was becoming concerned because I knew deep down in my heart that this man was increasingly controlling me with each passing day.

One day, the pressure of all of it just got too much. Even though I was afraid John would not like it, somehow I mustered up the guts to confront him, my own anger and frustration spilling out: *Why do you call me so much? I don't like it. It is weird that you are calling to check on me. I feel like you don't trust me. It is so embarrassing that my friends and family think it is not normal to be calling everywhere I go. They think you are freaking controlling me. Stop making me appear awful! I'm not lying to you, so please stop it. I'm at the location I tell you I'm at and you can trust that. Can you tell me why you are doing this to me? Because it's worrying me that all my friends and family have seen the same pattern, and it's making me really... sad and..."*

John looked at me with such viciousness in his eyes that I instantly stopped mid-sentence and just stared at him. He became enraged, shouting at me to shut up, that he checks on me because he loves me, to make sure I'm safe. That my family and friends are the ones who are crazy, and they don't love me, and on and on... Then he stomped out of the house, slamming the door hard.

Things got much worse after that. John dictated who I could speak to on the phone, who I visited and who could visit me. He acted so jealous and upset about everything that some of my friends stopped seeing me, and I got increasingly reluctant to see them or my family. He began to say vicious things, insulting me and telling me I wasn't worth it, even that I was worth*less*. Luis was becoming frightened of John and stayed away from him as much as he could.

It got to the point where I felt unable to speak at all because I was afraid of making him angry. With all his intrusions and phone calls all day, he made it really difficult for me to work anymore, so I quit my job.

Then I became pregnant. I was already seeing signs that John had also stopped being so nice to Luis. With his mood swings increasing and so quick to anger, he was acting meaner to my little boy. I was ready to take this verbal abuse, but it was painful to see it happening to my son.

But what could I do now? I was pregnant, I was trapped, and I felt like I had no choice but to stay.

Chapter Four

The Dream Unravels

I was so very ashamed of myself. I could hardly recognize the bright, happy, hopeful young woman I had been just a few years before. I did not like me or love me anymore. I no longer felt beautiful or worthy.

The dream life I had imagined with my Prince Charming was becoming a nightmare. I so wanted to believe that it was a bad dream, and day after day, I imagined I would wake up to the husband I had fallen in love with, laughing with my son, and enjoying my friends and my family.

I didn't want anyone to know that I was now being abused in some way every day, stuck in the house with no job, no social life, subject to whatever mood or whims John was feeling, becoming his target for insults, pushing and punching. I was suffering for my son, and it was painful for me to know that my little boy had to see his mother mistreated like this. John would sometimes hit Luis as well, and I tried to intervene when I could. But I was helpless to make a difference because when I stood up for us, it would only make him worse.

When we were with his family or friends, I would put on a happy smile, act as if everything was fine, and say nothing. If they asked me how I was, I said, *Fine... everything's good.* I knew I wasn't looking very good. I had gained weight, had dark circles under my eyes from stress and exhaustion, and couldn't even choose what I wanted to wear because John was in control of that too. When we were with others, John was his charming, funny, kind self – the man I remembered falling in love with and marrying.

It all seemed so impossible, yet this was becoming my reality every day.

The truth was that I was being subjected to mental, physical and verbal abuse regularly. I was beginning not to trust my own mind, beginning to believe that everything was my fault, to believe what he was telling me about myself – that I was ugly, fat, stupid and worthless. *When he was so nice to everyone else, how else could I understand why he was treating me so badly?* I must deserve this abuse because I did it to myself – he hated every mistake, every flaw, every time I tried to talk back or say the right thing. It must be all my fault.

My life no longer belonged to me. John was in full control of my entire life and my mind.

I never knew when he would come back from work or the club, just waiting to get angry and start a fight. If he didn't like what I cooked, he would throw the plate against the wall, yelling and calling me stupid and how I didn't even know how to cook. Sometimes I was so afraid of him that my heart would race and I would run to the bathroom to vomit or to just calm down my heart that was beating so fast I thought I could be having a heart attack (I later learned that what I was experiencing were panic attacks).

Then, just as suddenly, there would be one or two days out of the week when he would be happy – nice, charming, no problems. We would all go out for a ride or have dinner at a restaurant. Each time, I would hope this would be the time that would last, that he would be back to his old self and we would be happy again. But each time, he suddenly would go back to his abuser self, and it all would start up again. We would never know when it would start or how bad it was going to be.

My mind was being controlled, and I believed I had no power to call the police, nor could they do anything to help me anyway. After all, I was worthless. I was too ashamed to reach out to anyone else for help.

My mind became so confused and stressed that I couldn't see the magnitude of the control he had over me. I couldn't see that he had isolated me from anyone who could support me or help me. His plan was to trap me with him so he could control everything I did. And he was succeeding.

My mind couldn't see that he viewed me as weak and that he had created me to be a target for all his anger and hate and whatever he was suffering from. He became rude and mean, just picking a fight over anything and everything so he could take whatever it was out on me. I was his punching bag, and he did not care how he talked to or treated my son or me.

I believed that he was mentally ill, but I felt powerless to do anything about it. I was even afraid to do any research on mental illness in case he found out.

What I did see was that I was in a very bad situation and did not know what to do. I was scared and depressed. One day just followed after another. Often, I didn't even know what day it was. I went through the motions for the sake of Luis, getting him to school, clothed, and as safe as I could make his life.

When John was out of the house, often all night with this woman or that woman, I cried and cried, asking myself, *Why is this happening? Why does he want to hurt me? Why?* But there were no answers for me.

In my clearer moments, I knew I was living with a beast, a monster. I could not understand what I had done to make this man be so evil to us, but I had put myself into this situation, so I was the one to figure out how to come out of it.

How? I had no idea.

I began praying, day and night because I was so afraid. Since it was all my fault, what would God have me do? If I deserved this, should I accept my life and get used to living with this monster? I did not know, but I had faith and trust that there was an answer. And now God was giving me another child. There must be a reason, and I couldn't do anything but pray for God's answer. I prayed for the sake of my children, to give me the strength to bring this child into the world and to protect my son until I would be released from this situation – even if God's answer would cost me my life.

> *"You are my hiding place; You shall preserve me from trouble; You shall surround me with songs of deliverance...I will instruct you and teach you in the way you should go; I will guide you with My eye."* (Psalms 32:7-8 NKJV)

I waited as long as I could to tell John I was pregnant because I had no idea how he would react. What a relief it was that when I did tell him, he was VERY happy. He told me he was going to change and make sure that the baby would be healthy. He did try to be nice for the first few months of my pregnancy, being kinder to Luis and me and buying things for the baby.

He also told me to make sure it was a boy because he wanted a boy. *Just make sure it's a boy.* I would pray every day that the baby would be a boy. Soon it was time to get the ultrasound to find out the baby's health and gender. I made sure that I made the appointment when I knew John would be busy, in case it was a girl, and I went alone.

Sure enough, the technician confirmed to me that I was having a girl. *Are you sure??* I asked her. *Can you please double check?* She checked again, and said, *Yes, I am 100% sure that it's a girl!* I was SO happy because I wanted to have a girl, my princess! But soon, the fear crept in... I would have to tell John.

As soon as I got home, he asked me if I was having a boy, and I panicked – I just couldn't tell him. I said that they weren't sure yet, and we'll find out at the next appointment. I was that afraid of what he'd do, even though I knew he would find out eventually. I just couldn't think clearly.

At our five-month checkup, John insisted on going with me. I was so nervous I was shaking as we entered the doctor's office. She did the ultrasound, and John said, *So I want to find out our baby's gender. Is it a boy?* I froze. The doctor said, *No, I told your wife that she is having a girl!*

John stiffened and clenched his fists by his sides, the look on his face was frightening. He got so angry that he just went off on the doctor. I'm not even sure of what he was yelling, but I can still picture the shock on her face. I was so embarrassed. Then he turned on me: *You already KNEW it was a girl, but you hid it from me? Why did you hide it from me??* Shaking like a leaf, I blurted out, *Because if I told you it was a girl, you would be upset and you could hit me!*

He was furious and started railing on me, shouting mean things, calling me horrible names, making a scene that everyone in the room and in the waiting room could hear. The hospital staff just stared at us and looked at me as if they felt very sorry for me. If they only knew...

Even in that moment, I saw the sympathy for me on the faces of those people, yet I couldn't take it in, accept it or understand that I deserved it. I was too much in fear and shame to even think that someone here might be able to help me. All I could think of was that I had made a terrible mistake in lying to him, and right now, I just had to protect myself, my son and this little girl that was coming into the world.

John grabbed my arm and took me out of the hospital and to the car, yelling all the way as people just stopped and stared in shock. He drove home racing through the streets, swerving like a crazy person, continuing to shout at me, calling me names, accusing me of lying – and telling me that he *will not love my* daughter.

Still yelling and cursing loudly as we drove up to the house, he dropped me off and went back to work. That night, I cried in my room for hours, feeling so bad because I could not give him a boy – that's how strong the mind control was. It still hurts terribly today as I write this because I believed he was going to reject my daughter, the lovely princess I was carrying inside of me. I adored my daughter from the day I conceived her, just as I had adored my firstborn. It should have been a day of rejoicing, not of horror.

I got down on my knees and prayed again, this time asking God to calm my husband down so he wouldn't be too unhappy when he returned home after work, so that all of us could be safe.

Chapter Five

Frightening Patterns

There was a pattern to John's behavior. He would rage over the smallest thing, hit me or harm me in some way, stalk out of the house and stay away a few hours or overnight. Then, he would return home with all kinds of apologies, vowing he would not hurt me again. He offered me gifts so that I would forgive him. I would tell him I was sorry too so he would be nice to me, but I didn't mean it anymore.

Even from the beginning of our relationship, I had never wanted all the gifts he showered on me, and now, I hated being offered these things because it was all part of his deception – just another form of torture. I hid the gifts away, never using them, or whenever I had the chance, I would give them away to neighbors – these meaningless material things were just a reminder of my pain.

I believe that after the fateful doctor's visit, John may have gone to his family to talk to them, because he returned home, told me to shut up and just listen. Then he said he decided to accept that we were having a baby girl.

During the rest of the pregnancy, he left me alone, occasionally getting angry about how I had lied to him and taking the usual opportunities to tell me I was good for nothing, would never be anything in life, was stupid and worthless – what I'd been hearing now almost every day of my life with him.

John was hardly ever home now, and I knew he was cheating on me with different women. To be honest, I did not care. I hoped he would fall in love with someone else and leave me so I could be free.

———————

The wonderful day came when my princess was born. She was so beautiful and healthy! I kissed her and blessed her immediately, praying that her dad would love her and treat her kindly, and vowing that only God would know what her dad was putting me through.

Since I had a C-section, John was not there for the birth of his daughter but he came afterward to see her, and he seemed very happy. He stayed for a few hours and then left, telling me he was going to the club. The next day, a woman called to tell me that while I was in the hospital giving birth, she was having sex with John in our bed. I have no idea why she wanted to tell me this, and the truth was that I really didn't care what he did any-more. But it hurt just the same – another reminder that those rare moments of joy we had would only darken into sadness and evil and pain.

My beautiful new daughter, Karla Marie, and Luis were the joys of my life, and all that mattered now.

A few days later, John visited me again at the hospital, talking about the clubs he was attending and showing me a photo of one of the women dancers who performed there. I felt tired and weak and irritated by all his talk (knowing he was also having women in my bed while I was lying there recovering in the hospital), so I asked him, *Why are you talking about the club and showing me this picture? Why are you telling me all these things?*

In a flash, he turned dark and angry. He jumped up from the chair, grabbed the baby out of the bassinet, yelling that he was going to take her away, and rushed out of the room with her in his arms. I screamed until the nurse came in, and I shouted, *He's taking my baby!* The staff had already caught him in the hallway and demanded that he bring the baby back into the room or he would go to jail. I was so relieved I wept. Just as suddenly as he had exploded, John calmed down and apologized very charmingly in front of the staff. But I knew he was not sorry.

Once Karla and I were safely back home, things calmed down a little. I was thankful that John seemed to love our daughter. He was a little humble for a few weeks, telling me we were all going to be okay, that he was very sorry for hurting me, that he loved me, and he will change. I wanted to believe him, but I knew it was a lie and only a matter of time before he would be back to his abuser self.

For now, though, I felt such a wonderful feeling of peace, and I loved taking care of my little family. Luis was SO taken with this little princess, and it was fun to see that. He was such a good big brother, staying around Karla, always patting her gently, and making sure she was okay.

John was gone a lot during this time, which left our little family in peace. I was happy for the first time in a long time, feeling blessed by these moments the three of us had together. While John was home, we had to be very quiet, no talking loudly, no noises allowed, but at least we were not harmed.

During these couple of months, John seemed to be back to his old self, being nice to the people who lived in our building. But he was still in control of me, criticizing me for even saying 'hi' to a neighbor at the mailboxes or when we were out walking Karla. He warned me against getting involved in any conversation he was having with someone or getting into any conversations of my own with anyone. He was still watching my every move.

The thing is, John was not fooling anybody. They knew something was going on behind the closed doors of our apartment, with all the yelling, the crying, and the sounds of violence. They had to know the strange patterns of our lives:– me inside the house most of the time, his car gone for nights or days on end, me at his side silent and with fright in my eyes. Keeping control of me and my relationships with our neighbors wasn't going to hide his monstrous behavior.

What I know now is that the abuser has to keep up a false image of themselves and this perfect life they're leading to hide what is really going on within them. They can get very good at hiding those parts of their character that trigger their abusive side. But similar to an alcoholic, it becomes increasingly tougher to manage all the stories and the lies and the behavior. They can become more unhinged, more desperate – and more dangerous.

Slowly, I began to see him losing control of himself, and I began to realize that this wasn't just about me and the mistakes I was making and the worthless person he kept telling me that I was. I didn't understand the character of an abuser, but I could see the shifts happening to John that was disturbing to me and to the safety of my children.

One day, Dora, my next-door neighbor, saw John beating me out in the driveway near the car. She grabbed a broom, ran over, and smacked him with it, yelling: *Stop hitting that girl! Look how big you are – shame on you for hitting the mother of your kids! I will call 911 if you don't stop! You should be ashamed assaulting a woman!*

Real men don't hit no women! Real men protect their women! She grabbed my hand and took me into her apartment, leaving him standing there stunned.

Oh, my! How relieved I was that someone actually saw my life and had noticed! That he was not in control for a few moments, exposed as the monster he truly was. But relief quickly turned to terror because...*what do I do now?* My kids are in the house, and what will *happen when I go home?* Dora kindly let me hide at her house until it got dark. I was so afraid to go back, and I had no idea how I would get into the apartment. I knew he would find a way to blame me, and I was afraid of this 6-ft-5 man and what he was capable of doing.

Dora tried to convince me to call the police or leave him, but my kids were in the apartment so I told her I had to go back. When I finally went back home, I found that the door was unlocked. I tiptoed in, desperately hoping he was asleep or out somewhere. All the lights were off, and I quietly, carefully made my way into the bedroom.

Where have you been all this time?! I jumped, and my heart stopped. He was sitting in the bedroom in the dark, waiting for me. *I was just visiting at Dora's,* I replied softly, staying near the door and not daring to get any closer. But he interrupted and went into a yelling fit, blaming me for what happened, and on and on. I just kept apologizing, agreeing with everything he said, promising to make sure that Dora would never get involved in our lives and saying anything that would make him calmer. It was harrowing, but he never touched me. I waited for him to calm down and checked on the kids to make sure they were safe.

I hated to lie, I hated myself, and I hated being in the agony of not knowing from one moment to the next if I would live or die – that any day could be the end of my life.

Chapter Six

The Darkest Days

Learning to deal with an abusive partner is difficult at first, but you ultimately adapt to the abuse and learn to cope with suffering. When you understand who this monster is and what he is capable of doing to you, not only physically but mentally, you get into a type of permanent survival mode – learning his patterns, getting a good idea of what triggers him, and knowing what to say to calm him down or not beat you more. You do whatever you can to handle every situation so you do not go insane or kill yourself. That is a reality of this life.

When I say John wasn't fooling anybody, what's also true is... neither was I.

Often, when I was allowed to go out to the store, to take the kids somewhere or to church, I would have to wear sunglasses to hide my black eye. I would put on a lot of makeup to hide the bruises on my face. Sometimes my body hurt so much from being thrown to the floor or shoved against the wall that I was barely able to walk without pain.

At church, it sometimes felt like all eyes were on me in my sunglasses or heavy makeup, and the shame was almost unbearable. No one ever said anything, but I knew God was listening. My sunglasses hid my tears as well as my black eye as I prayed and begged God to help me out of this chaotic life. All I wanted was to be in a secure place with my kids, but I didn't know who to ask – even at church – because it was taboo to defy or divorce your man. I was too embarrassed and ashamed of my life to tell anyone.

And it is more complicated than just not telling someone. As I look back, probably several people tried to help, but we were fighting against a monster. They meant well, but either I couldn't allow myself to hear them, or they didn't know what I was dealing with and what constant danger my kids and I were in.

Where we were living then was too far away from my family to help me. Mom was a wise mother and knew that something was wrong with her daughter. After not hearing from me for many months, she had my brother call the police to ask them to come check on me.

When the police knocked on the door, John opened it, and they asked for me. I had no idea what was going on, as I had never contacted them. The officers stood outside on the steps. I came to the door, and they asked if I was okay. I said I was fine, adding, *May I ask why are you here?* They told me that my mother phoned them because she was worried about me and wanted to know why I hadn't called her. I must not have been very convincing, because they asked me a few more times and in different ways if I was okay and, with John standing behind me, all I could say was, *I'm fine*. Finally, I thought to say that my phone was broken, but that as soon as I fixed it, I would contact her.

The officers went away, and my husband released his rage. He began doing what he did best: hitting me. Then he dragged me to the bedroom, threw me on the bed, and pressed a pillow over my face for so long I almost stopped breathing. At what felt like the last moment of my life, he let go and stormed out of the room. I laid there weakly, trying to catch my breath. I had so many blood spots – contusions – on my face that I looked like I had chickenpox. It was terrible, but I thank God I was able to breathe again.

And I said a prayer of gratitude to my mom and brother for trying to help – it gave me comfort to know that I wasn't totally alone.

After what John did to me, I knew that everything John and I ever had between us was gone, blown away like ashes in the wind. Sometimes, I couldn't even remember those early days of living with my Prince Charming. Sometimes, I couldn't even remember who I WAS before I met him.

For many years now, I was regularly being humiliated and mistreated. I was fat. I didn't care how I looked. I would eat at night when he went to bed. I kept away from him as much as possible while doing my duties as a wife. I learned to keep a fake smile on my face and pretend to be happy no matter what was going on, no matter how depressed I was. I was never able to have a deep sleep. I had to wake up every day next to a man who made me wonder if this was the day that would be my last.

The only things I cared about were my beautiful children. I learned how to survive, knowing that I had these kids to love and protect. The only joy I remember during these times was seeing my children safe, praying to God to protect me and grant me life, not for myself but to ensure that my children would have the safe and loving life that I could give them.

Often, I felt defeated, but I never gave up fighting for my kids and for my freedom!! My life was full of uncertainty. But deep, deep inside, I refused to believe that there was no hope or no better future as long as I could survive. I began to pray more and more; GOD was my only refuge. I read the Bible to learn of His promises, hear the comforting words, and know that one day He would rescue me from the hands of this evil man.

I wanted to flee, but my mind wasn't ready yet. I was enslaved by my husband, and there was no place in my imagination to see a way to escape. For so many years, I was told that I was nothing without him, that no one cared for me, or would ever love me as much as he did. No one reached out to me; I had no idea where my family was, and I was afraid to try to contact them. I didn't understand anything; all I knew was that I was used to being abused and this was my life right now with no chance of escape.

John had lost his job (I never knew why) and had just started a new job as a security guard. He was feeling very powerful because he was issued a gun which he carried everywhere. For some reason, he was getting even meaner, and there was no relationship or civility between us anymore. I rarely went anywhere, we didn't go out together very often, and he was out a lot. Karla was around six months old, so I had my hands full with the two children with little time for socializing. I still had no car, so I was dependent on him to help me with the kids and do the shopping we needed.

One morning, he came home late from work and looked very tired. I knew he'd finished his shift hours ago, so I asked him, *Why didn't you come home right after you were finished working?* He didn't respond, and I asked again, *Why are you late? Did anything special happen at work?*

I already knew the answer. I had overheard the radio walkie-talkie conversations from the other workers about

John leaving with a woman. I was getting so tired of this, hurt and angry that everybody knew what he was doing. Tired of putting up with his cheating and disrespect.

Something made me confront him this time.

He immediately flew into a rage, shouting at me that all he does is work hard to give me everything, and calling me names and curse words. I instantly regretted ever asking him. I told him I was very sorry. Then he took it further, going a little insane with making up stories about how people are lying about him, he's just working hard for me and the kids, he doesn't know why they're talking about him, all he's doing is his job.

I knew he was lying because he had introduced me to some of these ladies who I knew he was seeing. When we did go out together, I saw him being very pleasant and charming to them (I remembered how charming he could be). I watched him walk them to their cars, using a different voice than he used with me. He was a different person with them and doing it right in front of me like a taunt when he never talked to me that way anymore.

I was just his enemy, his target, his punching bag, a body producing a child for him.

I was thinking this when I said to him, *I wish you were kind and nice to me like you are to the rest of the people.* He looked at me, eyes wide as if I had just slapped his face, and his anger went up two more notches. He became really unglued, shouting, who was I to dare to tell him how to talk to me or anyone else? I was lucky to be with him and he couldn't care less how I was feeling, and on and on in a frightful way I'd never seen before.

Then, suddenly, he grabbed a large glass statue standing near him and hurled it straight at me. It hit my left arm, sending a stabbing pain through my body. I dropped to my knees in agony. He called an ambulance to take me to the hospital, helped me inside it, but sent me to the hospital alone.

At the ER, the doctor, of course, asked me how it happened, and I was afraid to tell him the truth. I could not let him or anyone else know that my husband had thrown a heavy object at me. I did not have the power to tell on him.

Several hours later, I got discharged. In the cab, on the way home, fear surged up in me again. *What would I find at home? What would my husband be like?* My stomach tightened and my heart beat faster, like they always did, as I mentally prepared for whatever might happen when I entered the house.

When I arrived at our building, Sam, the maintenance manager, saw me coming up the stairs and stopped me, asking: *Why is your arm all wrapped up? Are you okay, Ana? You look like you've been crying. Did anyone hurt you?*

I told him that I was coming from the hospital because I had fallen and hurt my arm, and I thanked him for his concern. I knew he didn't believe me for a second. I knew he knew I was being abused, and Sam looked at me with eyes that said, *Don't lie to me, Ana.* I wanted so badly to tell him what was happening, but I could not open my mouth.

I can't really understand or explain why I was so afraid to tell anyone about my situation. I just couldn't imagine the risk of John finding out. I saw now what he was capable of – and that he had a gun. What would he do to me, or to my kids?

The decision was to suffer in silence, at least for now, until I got an answer to my prayers.

This was a period where I kept trying to understand why this was happening. I kept turning questions over and over in my mind, like: *How do we meet people? We don't meet them by accident, right? Everyone is meant to cross our path for a reason. What was the reason that John and I had crossed paths?*

I believe we all go through something in life for a reason, that God has a purpose for us. I thought my path was to have a normal and good husband who would love me and I would love him, that we would have a family, have happiness and do good things in the world. I did not like my life during these years, and I was searching to make some kind of sense out of it all.

I felt shame for not seeing the signs of what John was like and what was becoming of me. I wanted to just go away where he would never find me, but my self-esteem was so low that I didn't believe in me. I couldn't imagine anyone helping me, only judging, criticizing, wondering why I was staying, and saying, *Why don't you just leave him?*

What many don't understand is that you may want to leave, but you don't know how. Day after day for seven years, your brain has been told that you are unlovable, you are worthless, this is what you deserve, you are nothing without this guy – *and if you leave him, he will cut up your face to the point that no one will ever be with you again.*

And here is the most difficult part: You begin to get used to the dysfunctional marriage. It becomes your new normal. It becomes normal to be abused either verbally, physically, or mentally, to be controlled and to suffer. You are not sure anymore that you could even be in a healthy marriage or have a happy life.

These were my darkest days. I began to wake up each morning asking if my life was worth living. Asking why? Why does this person not see me as someone to love? Why is he so horrible to me? Where is his mercy and decency?

I will admit to you that I did have some dark moments when I did not want to live anymore, when I asked God to take my life along with my children's.

Chapter Seven

The Man I Once Knew Is Gone

There was one night that was so rough I did call the police myself. They came to the house, and I guess what was happening was pretty obvious because John went to jail for the night. The police were very nice to me and helped me get a room at a good hotel for myself and the kids. I was able to stay there for a few days while we waited for a spot at a domestic violence women's shelter.

I was grateful to be safe for the moment, but I hadn't brought anything with me, including any money – *how would I feed my kids?* It was such a humiliating experience, but I had no choice but to go down to the hotel restaurant and ask the host if it was possible to feed my kids because they were hungry.

He replied, *Sure, not only can your kids eat, but you can too.* I had tears in my eyes as I thanked him. I was so embarrassed to have to beg for food. To this day, I am still thankful for the meals he kindly provided us.

The time came to go to the shelter, and we stayed there for a couple of weeks. Then I found out I was pregnant. I didn't know what to do. John's voice was in my head, telling me over and over that I'd never get a job because I had no connections and no skills. I was thinking, *Who is going to hire a pregnant lady? How was I going to find a place to live, pregnant and with two kids?*

I did not believe that I could possibly make this work. Even my sister-in-law told me I was crazy to stay with him and offered to help me, but my brain was so damaged I couldn't believe that I could overcome this situation. John had put so much garbage in my head that I did not know how to go back to a normal life in a normal world.

The only way I knew was to go back to him. You may not understand why – and neither did I.

I called John, told him I was pregnant, and asked him to forgive me for putting him in jail, to please take me back because I did not know what to do.

So, I went back to him.

———————

I think John was surprised that I would take the action to call the police because he really seemed to be trying to be nice. Once again, he told me he would change, that he didn't want to lose me, didn't want to lose his family. I believed 10% of what he was saying, but I felt the tiniest bit more empowered that I could have had any kind of effect on him by standing up for myself.

Another factor that made a difference in the way he was acting was that this time, I was going to have a little boy. He was very happy about that. It didn't stop the abuse, but there were more days between the ugliness because he was happy and a little kinder to Luis and Karla.

A few days later, John was out, and someone called him. I was instructed never to answer the phone, so I let the voice message run. Then, taking a chance, I listened to the message. The call was from a man whose voice I didn't recognize. He was giving John instructions on how to use "the pills" he was providing for him. It was clear that this man was not a doctor or a pharmacist and identified himself as a "friend" but gave no name.

I didn't know anything about any pills or reasons why my husband might need them. Maybe this was the problem with his mood swings. Maybe this was why his behavior was so crazy sometimes – and getting worse.

In that moment, I knew that the man who had once been good to me, who would buy me anything, who was proud that I was at his side, who wanted to be with me always – that man did not exist anymore.

Around this time, we moved across the country to live with John's parents as our new home wasn't ready for us to move into it yet. They had always been kind to me and the kids, and I was so grateful to be with other people again, feeling a little less trapped by this monster. It was an uncomfortable situation because I didn't know what they knew, and I was still very afraid to say anything to them or to ask for help. John seemed to be controlling himself more, so I had no black eyes or bruises that his parents could see.

During this time, Isabel, my step mother-in-law, was visiting me while John was at work. She noticed how many clothes her stepson had in his closet. She peeked into my closet, which was almost empty, and commented on that to me. I didn't know what to say. She said that it was okay to go shopping for me and for the kids. She looked at me in a sincere way and encouraged me to be strong. She told me *not to be afraid of him.*

Isabel did not know all that was going on in our household or how her stepson was cheating on me – and I didn't tell her – but she sensed something was wrong. I was very grateful to her for encouraging me and supporting me like this. I hung onto that little glimmer of hope that she had sparked in me.

We moved into our new home a few weeks later.

When my birthday came along, John surprised me with an overnight stay at a five-star hotel nearby, arranging for the kids to be with their grandparents and making dinner reservations at an elegant restaurant. When I entered our hotel room, I was amazed to find it filled with beautiful flowers! He also gave me the gift of a gym membership.

I knew it was his way of telling me he was sorry, but I was so sad inside because it meant nothing to me anymore – he was just being nice because his guilt was nagging at him. Still, it was a few moments of peace (I couldn't say happiness), and I embraced every single one of those moments. It was a day to remember, as it reminded me of when we first met.

After that, John actually allowed me to go to the gym whenever I wanted to, and I was thrilled. I was finally able to go somewhere by myself, and I went every day – for a while.

One day, as I was walking the treadmill, I overheard two girls talking next to me. One was talking all about how she was dating a guy and getting into all the details – how much she loved him and what he looked like and that he bought her a car and on and on. With my still-poor English I couldn't catch it all, but it soon became crystal clear that the guy she was talking about was my husband!

I could feel my face getting red and feeling angrier as she went on. I was shouting inside, *What are you talking about? I'm right here and you must know who I am – how dare you? And here's my husband telling me he doesn't want to lose me, and he's with you and buying you a car?* Of course, I knew he lied to me all the time and I really did wish he'd just leave me. But it still felt like one more humiliation, yet another dagger in my heart. And now I had to see this girl every time I was at the gym, knowing she was sleeping with him, and they both were probably laughing at me behind my back.

The whole experience poisoned my desire to go to the gym. I still went a couple of days a week because I was determined to get out of the house and take care of myself. But every time I saw either of the girls there, I felt embarrassed and humiliated and tried to avoid them. Then I discovered that John was following me there and watching me from outside, for who-knows-what reason.

He couldn't stop himself. His patterns were ramping up again – controlling me, getting mad at me, then apologizing and saying he didn't want to lose me, over and over (all the while, cheating on me and harming me). I would say all the right things to calm him down, but inside I felt anxious and worried that he was hiding his craziness, and it was only a matter of time before it would explode.

———

One day. early in my pregnancy, John told me we were going to the city for dinner that evening. So, I dressed up, and off we went. Along the way, he stopped for gas and I asked him if I could use the bathroom. He said okay, so I went inside the store of the gas station to use their restroom.

As I was walking back to the car, a man who had followed me out of the store, came up alongside me and said, *Hello...hello, miss – I'd like to talk to you, please.* I froze and said to him while stepping up my pace toward the car, *Uh, yes, what do you want?* He began to say how beautiful I was, how exotic. Oh no! I got super nervous! I thanked him and hurried to get into the car, knowing John would probably be angry seeing me with this man.

The guy followed behind me until I got inside the car. Then he tapped on the driver's side window until John rolled it down. *Hello,* the man said, *Is this your wife?* John nodded. The man then looked at me and said, *I am a photographer and I have an agency for models. You would be perfect for my team because you have a beautiful and exotic Latina look. I would like to have a photo session with you, and I could put your pictures in magazines.*

I replied, *Thank you very much,* and looked down, not knowing what else to say. I was very nervous about what was happening and what John might do next. The truth was that I also was stunned and flattered. *Wasn't I fat and ugly?* I hadn't heard any kind words like that in a long, long time! It pleased me that a man spoke highly of me and thought I was beautiful. Whoever he was, I was grateful for that moment of light. I would hang onto those words for months, especially whenever John insulted me cruelly.

At this point, John was talking to the man, promising that he would take me to the studio as soon as we could schedule it. The man gave him his business card and said to me, *Please try to come in the next week or so, so we can get you ready for this new adventure. You'll love it, and I know we can give you some great opportunities.* I just smiled and stayed silent because I knew John was lying to him and would never allow me to do such a thing.

Oh, my! We drove away and I could literally feel his anger get bigger and bigger – but he didn't say a word to me. I was very nervous and couldn't stop shaking all the way to the city. We had a quick drink, then John told me he didn't feel too good and wanted to head back home.

We drove in silence for a while – and then he started: *Why was this man talking to you? What did you say to him? Why were you flirting with him?* No matter what I said, he kept at it, raising his voice and sounding menacing. *You were flirting with him! You were talking to him like you knew him! Why did he feel he could just approach you like that?* Shaking, I finally said, *I don't know why he followed me. I said nothing to him, I just wanted to get to the car. He thought I looked pretty and maybe I need to hear that because I haven't heard it in such a long time.* I stopped and held my breath – what had I just said?? John got quiet and we drove the rest of the way home in silence, but I knew he was upset.

I was upset too and happy for our silence. I realized that the tiny sparks that were showing light on my situation – the hospital staff's sympathy, my neighbor Dora's help, my family's offers of support, the maintenance man's caring inquiry, my mother-in-law's encouragement, this stranger's flattering words – were growing into a flame inside me that was giving me strength.

Even with all the mental abuse messing up my brain, I was beginning to understand John's real story and his sickness. I was beginning to get clear about my responsibility to my children and our future, to what mattered most – and that included ME and not him or my marriage.

These were baby thoughts that were sneaking into my brain every so often. Then they would fly away just as quickly as my reality of regular abuse would set in again. I still could not be me. I knew it was best to keep my mouth shut and keep myself as invisible as possible.

We pulled up to the house without a word. John jumped out of the car and slammed it with all his muscle – something he did often because he knew it always made the kids and me jump with fright. He immediately went upstairs and I followed him inside. In a few minutes, the phone rang several times and since John always answered the phone right away, I finally answered it myself. It was one of his friends, asking if it was okay with me if John helped him change the tire of his car. I'd been here before – I knew what was going on. This time, something made me say, *Mike, don't lie to me. John just called you and told you to call me with an excuse so he can go cheat on me with his girlfriend. Tell him he can go ahead – I don't care.*

I hung up the phone, a little bit shocked at myself, but it felt good to take control for a change, to call out the lie we were living. I was worried about what would happen next, but I made myself scarce, and a few moments later, I heard the door slam as John went out.

He did not come home for several days this time. I remember my father-in-law being so kind, sitting with me and the kids, reading to us. He told me that he was very sorry and didn't say anything more. I told him not to worry, that I would be okay.

And I actually started to believe it.

Chapter Eight

Enough!

I was seven months pregnant, sitting at home alone, the kids were with their grandparents. A phone rang suddenly, and I realized it was John's cellphone which he must have forgotten when he left for work. I went over to the phone, where the caller was leaving a voice message, and I saw that the profile image on the screen was a woman.

In that moment, something just snapped inside me. *Enough! Enough!!* I called the number back, found out who she was and where she worked. Before I could change my mind, I grabbed my cellphone, called a cab and went straight to her workplace. I saw her on the street, on her way back to work from lunch. Somehow, she knew who I was (had she been in my bed when I wasn't there?) and she called, *Hello!* as she approached me with a smile, then she said: *Oh, did your husband tell you about us?* I replied, *About "US"? NO, he did not. I'm here to find out what is going on here!*

She went on to tell me that they have been together for a while and that he was going to leave me for her. All the while, she had this broad smile on her face, practically laughing as she looked at my swollen belly. I started to cry with frustration, anger, humiliation, everything building up from all these years, as she went on and on about how much she loves him and what fun they have. I couldn't take it anymore, and I did something I've never done in my life – I slapped her! Before she could do or say one more thing, I turned and walked away.

I immediately called John, who, of course, denied everything, making up ridiculous stories and trying to act angry and turn it back on me. I hung up and went home, crying and shaking – only to find the police at my door.

This woman had the nerve to call the police on me for assault. Really? You have been sleeping with a married man whose wife is seven months pregnant, and I'm the bad guy here?

I answered the policeman's questions absolutely honestly and in tears. I was shaking badly and feeling so much pain in my stomach picturing her enjoying the moment, laughing in my face, when she knew a baby was inside me, showing not a bit of compassion or any consideration that I was pregnant. Inside I was about to break down, not believing this – all of it – was actually happening to me.

Gratefully, the officer was very understanding, and decided to speak to my husband. I can imagine the lies John told him, but all I know is that the whole thing went away, and I was never charged.

But the damage was done. I began to feel very sick and weak. In the weeks that followed, I was at the doctor's office every Friday because the baby was not doing well and they needed to monitor me regularly. I was instructed to take it easy and be on bed rest.

I believe they continued their affair because I hardly saw John during the last two months of my pregnancy. I thanked God for this blessing because it was such a relief that no one was yelling or pushing me around day after day.

This period also gave me time to think, to remember and to realize for the first time and in a new way that I was living with an enemy in my own home.

I thought about:

...when he would do anything to find an excuse to take out his anger on me, like put a piece of trash in the middle of the floor so he could complain, call me names, tell me I'm no good, hit me, and continue the fight with Karla or Luis.

...when he grabbed my beautiful seven-year-old daughter under her arms, lifted her up and pushed her against the wall, yelling at her like a crazy man. She was so frightened that she peed on herself.

...when he would create all these rules for the house as if he were daring us to break them – every can in the pantry had to be in a perfect position, the pasta in a certain place, cereal in a certain place, all in perfect order, or we would get into trouble. He regularly called me too stupid to buy groceries or cook properly.

And the day he came home early from his shift very upset about something that happened at work, he started on me, *The house is a mess! What the hell do you do all day here? Do you do anything?*

I said, *I clean, I cook, I do laundry, I take care of the kids, the pantry is organized. So I don't know why you are upset – I have not done anything wrong.*

He told me to shut up and kept up the complaining and getting more and more worked up. Suddenly, he pulled out his gun, pointed it at my head and pulled the trigger. For one terrifying moment, I truly thought my life was over.

But...Silence. Nothing happened. For some reason, the trigger stuck and the bullet did not come out. I knew in that moment that God had intervened.

In the next moment, we heard a loud knock on the door. We both stopped, frozen. John quickly put his gun away and went to open the door. It was Marcos, his boss, who heard all the yelling and came by to find out what was going on. He told John to stop treating me like this.

John began to calm down and I slowly realized the most frightening experience of my life had just passed. It was a strange moment because it was like Marcos came out of nowhere – he lived nearby but had never for once come to visit. He may never know how grateful I am that he took the time to intervene.

———————

The day had come for my son to be born. I was supposed to be at the hospital at 5:00 am, and I was worried that I wouldn't make it because John had been out all night and had not come home yet. I did not know what to do. I remembered my sister-in-law said she would help me with the kids and I was about to call her to come get me, but he showed up at the last minute and took me to the hospital. I did not say a thing on the way because I needed to be okay for my new son.

The baby came and everything went great, the hospital staff was amazing, and I received beautiful flowers, which was so nice. Three days later, Johnny David and I were discharged, and my husband drove us home.

My husband dropped us off and left, and was out most of the time after, leaving me home alone to recover and take care of the three kids.

About a week later, I started to feel sick. I was not healing right from the surgery and was in so much pain around the incision that I called John to take me to the hospital. He came, but was very upset, driving fast over speed bumps and potholes, which made my discomfort even worse.

I was admitted into the hospital and stayed there for seven days to recover from a serious infection. To my memory, my husband did not visit me one day that I was there. Back at home, the kids looked like they were okay (grateful that his family probably helped with them); I was relieved to be back with my children. And I was on my way to another kind of recovery – I was getting my answers from God.

I started to think of a plan to leave my husband.

It was going to be hard to do with three young kids and it all felt very scary. Even knowing I had family that would help me with money to start over, when I tried to even imagine escaping, my entire body would shake just at the idea that he would find me. I knew it was possible that he could kill me because he had already tried more than once.

I believe emotional abuse is even worse than physical abuse. You can heal a broken arm or a black eye, but how do you heal a broken mind and a broken heart?

I continued to pray every day, not knowing how or when, but I knew a day of joy was coming. I would talk to myself, repeating it again and again: ***One day is coming when I will be free, I will get back to be me again. One day I will be happy with just my kids and me.***

Chapter Nine

An Angel Comes to Help

One day out of the blue (or was I being sent an angel?), I got a call from my friend, Wendy. She must have called my Mom to get my number. I was so surprised because I had not talked to her in years!

When she asked how I was doing, I did not know what to say to her. She knew me as a happy, outgoing person and she recognized my silence. She picked up right away that I was not the same person she had known, and she told me she was worried. She asked again, *Are you okay?* I said, *Yes, I am okay.* I couldn't help but hear the sadness in my own voice.

I really wanted to tell her what I was going through, but it was her first time calling me after so long, and it felt too soon to just open up and dive into it all. *Where would I even begin?* And I was carrying so much embarrassment and shame I couldn't bear for her to know. So, we spoke for a few minutes and hung up.

Wendy tried calling me again, and I was too depressed to pick up the phone. But she did NOT give up. She kept checking on me regularly, leaving me messages. I was grateful that she was in my life and supporting me, but I did not want her to know anything about my life – I had nothing good to share with her or brag about or be proud about. But she kept on calling until one day she left this message: *I know you are suffering. Please answer my calls or call me when you are alone so we can talk. I want to help you.*

I answered her next call, and we did talk. She became my angel, helping me to repair my broken brain.

Wendy lived in Kansas and I lived on the East Coast, but she would constantly remind me that I was not alone, and after a while of her repeating that, I started to feel it was true. She checked in to make sure I was safe. She would tell me how strong I was, how beautiful and intelligent I was. At first, it was shocking to hear such kind words and hard for me to receive them. She would regularly remind me of the me from childhood, the Ana she used to know – and slowly, I began to remember her too. I started to beg my brain to open up and see a little light at the end of this dark, infernal tunnel.

She didn't give up, and in slow, tiny, baby steps, I began to gain strength and believe in myself. I will always be grateful for Wendy's love and care and patience (we remain friends to this day).

Little did I know, I was going to need every bit of the strength and faith I could find inside me.

————————

My determination was growing, but I couldn't yet get my brain clear to make a plan. My desperation was growing too as John began to get increasingly violent. More than once, I ran out of the house, desperate to get away from him, but I never succeeded.

One time, I ran to the car, which was parked in front of the house. I managed to get inside and tried to start the car, but he was faster than me. He kicked in the window and the glass shattered all over my face and body. He snatched me out of the car, yelling at me and dragging me inside the house by my dress. Inside, he pushed me to the floor, grabbed a big jug of water and poured it on top of my head.

I cried and begged him to stop, but he then dragged me across the floor all over the house until my dress ripped apart. The kids saw everything, which was the most painful part of it all for me watching my kids see what he was doing to me.

I truly don't know whether or not he ever felt bad when he hurt me. I guess I will never know.

————————

For a little while, John's dad hired both of us to work for him at his company. I think now that John was probably against the idea, but what could he say to his dad? I was grateful to be doing something useful and making money, but the experience every day at work was horrible. Now his control over me was happening day and night. He was watching me all the time, just waiting for me to make a mistake or say something wrong or dare to talk to someone. And, of course, I had to hand all my paychecks over to him and only saw enough money to keep the kids fed and the electricity on.

One Friday, his dad paid me for an entire half-year in advance...to this day, I wonder if perhaps he did this to help his grandchildren and me get away from John. I didn't think that at the time, just put the money in my purse, and forgot about it until later that evening when my husband burst into the room, super angry, and shouting, *Why are you hiding things from me?* Surprised because I could never hide anything from him when he was watching me all the time, I responded, *What do you mean? I am not hiding anything from you!* He pushed me hard and said, *Why are you hiding the fact that Dad paid you in advance?* I told him because I thought his dad would tell him, and I was sorry I forgot the mention it on the way home. I didn't know he would get so mad.

It all felt so ridiculous – just too much, and I ran out of the house just to get away from him. He followed me out and caught me, grabbed me, picked me up, and carried me back inside the house and up to the bedroom. He threw me on the bed and put a pillow over my face, holding it down and screaming like a crazy man, calling me a stupid B.... F... B... and repeating again and again not to ever hide anything from him. I tried to fight back to defend myself, but it was hopeless because he was so strong. He did not stop until I lost my strength and lay limp. Then he took the pillow off my face and walked out of the bedroom.

Chapter Ten

Escape

While I continued to take the abuse, I was plotting my escape. I didn't know exactly how or when, but I was ready to take the chance. I saw no other choice, and this "new" reality strengthened me.

One night, my step mother-in-law Isabel called and asked how I was doing. This time, I told her exactly how it was going. I explained my situation to her. She said she would help me if I ever decided to leave. I thanked her, and hung up the phone crying with joy because I believed that God had answered my prayers in that moment.

Late one night, later that same week, when I was sleeping, I woke up suddenly because I felt someone touch my shoulder. I heard a voice saying everything was going to be okay. I jumped out of bed, terrified because I thought it was John and he was going to kill me. I rushed to his room, but he was sleeping. I calmed down and felt peace inside. I felt like an angel had come to visit me while I was sleeping.

I saw that it was time to act and simply escape.

A week later, the opportunity of a lifetime presented itself. On this night, John was very upset with me for whatever reason. He had a machete in his hand and was slamming it on the floor over and over and over, telling me he was going to hurt me. I was terrified, so weak I could hardly breathe with the thought of what he could do to me. And I was scared to think of how he could harm us all if he found out I was planning to flee with the kids.

I was faced with two terrible choices. Both felt scary, but at the same time, I somehow knew that this was my deliverance day.

How would I escape? I had thought of a plan, but suddenly couldn't think clearly. My head felt like it was going to explode as he kept pounding the floor with the machete. I tried to be as quiet and invisible as I could. He finally stopped, dropped the machete, and went outside to smoke a cigarette.

This was my chance! I remembered what I'd plan to do if the chance ever came. I made up my mind to trust in the Lord and do it. I dialed 911 and hung up the phone. I pulled the cord out of the wall because I knew the police would call back and ask questions. And I knew that they would just show up at this address without me having to speak to them or to John... as long as they came in time.

Nervous, shaking and heart pounding, I ran to the bathroom and locked myself inside, listening at the door, hoping and praying that the police would come before

John came back inside and noticed the phone was not connected and then hunt me down.

I jumped when I heard the knock on the front door. I could hear him go to the door, and he immediately started shouting. I heard the police speaking to him, but he kept shouting and shouting nonstop, sounding crazy and out of control. I came quietly out of the bathroom and toward the door, when one of the officers spotted me and said quietly, *You need to leave RIGHT NOW. Your husband is very upset, and you could die here tonight.*

I asked them to please give me a few minutes to pick up some clothes for the kids and me, and I grabbed what I could as they told me to hurry. It was difficult because I had no idea where I was going, no money, no job, no skill, no self-esteem, no identity. Luis was helping me grab things for us when he saw me stop for a moment.

It suddenly felt like a heavy weight was crushing my body, and I said softly, *I can't leave because I don't have anything.* Luis came over to me, touched my hand, and said, *You believe in God, so don't be afraid. Let's go, Mom, God will help us.*"

That was all I needed to hear. That simple statement from my beautiful son was a message from God to give me the strength that I needed so I could have the courage to leave.

I can still see the look on my husband's face as he threatened me, saying I would regret this and other things I can't remember, as the police were insisting I go with them NOW, and the four of us ran to our car to go to the police station.

On the way to the police station, tears of pain and fear were streaming down my face because I had no idea what was going to happen to us. Beautiful Luis kept saying to me all the way there, *Yes, Mom, you did it! Do not cry – it's okay. We are safe now. We're free now, Mom! Just please, please, this time, do not go back. He is not going to change. Please don't believe anything he says or promises he makes. He will kill you, Mom, if you stay with him. I love you, Mom. God will help us!*

So grateful to my son in those moments, I said, *Yes, hijo, we are safe and free now.* I looked back at Luis with little Johnny in his arms and Karla huddled and crying in the backseat. We prayed together in that car, and I promised them that I would never go back, that I would make sure that we stayed together always.

"I can do all things through Christ who strengthens me." (Philippians 4:13 NKJV)

Chapter Eleven

A New Life Begins

At the police station, I called my dear step mother-in-law Isabel and told her that we escaped. She sent someone to the station to hand me $500 in cash. We got a hotel room for a couple of nights. I was so very grateful, but not yet relaxed or sure of what was going to happen next.

Isabel asked me to find an apartment and said that she would arrange to pay for the first month and security. The four of us got to the apartment – with no bed, no chairs, no blankets, no pillows, no dishes and no money to buy anything. But... we had each other! We looked at each other in amazement and in love, realizing that now we could talk and laugh and jump and twirl and dance – and BE!

Every few hours, I would sneak looks out the window to see if he was going to be outside waiting in the car, watching like he had so many, many times before. It was so hard to believe that this was happening, that he wasn't present in our lives every moment, that the torture might finally be over.

Then, on the second day, I *did* see him drive by our place! I instantly called Isabel and told her he'd found us (we learned later that the management company had sent a thank-you card for the rental to his home, so he knew our address). She said, *Let me see what I can do and I will call you back.*

Those next two hours were the longest two hours ever as I feared for the safety of my kids. But her call came, and she had found a way for us to stay with one of her daughters. I thanked her so gratefully and we went to their house until I could get back on my feet again.

It felt good to be in a house that actually had furniture and an indescribable sense of... normalcy! I felt safe there, and the kids were happy that they could go outside and play. I felt relieved, but I was always watching my back to make sure no one was following us.

I got the kids back in school and started to put our lives in some kind of order. It wasn't easy because everything had been taken from me. Once I had lived in elegance with celebrities, beautiful clothes, travel and luxury. Now, all my possessions fit into one small plastic grocery bag that I had grabbed frantically while the police were waiting.

While my kids were in school, I would sometimes just sit alone in my room, full of so many feelings of uncertainty, fear and deep sadness. I felt like a failure because I had gotten myself into such a disaster. I could barely imagine my future or what life could look like without him. But then my mind would clear a little, and I would remember that we were FREE and I was now solely responsible for my children. Then I would tell myself over and over to be strong – even though I didn't exactly know what that meant because my strength had been taken from me for so long.

One thing I would always come back to amid all these emotions: I KNEW I could never go back to him, no matter what. I would keep my promise to Luis. I knew that I had to stand up for myself because no one else would – it was up to me. I called on my strength and resolve as much as I could to move forward. And I continued to pray for all of us.

As soon as I was able, I started to hustle to find a job. I didn't know where to start because I had no skills – not even a high school diploma in this country – and I didn't know anyone anymore who I could call. Then my prayers were answered again. One day when I picked up Karla at elementary school, she was with her friend, and the friend introduced me to her mom. We talked for a while, and I asked her if she knew anything about a job.

Yes, she said, *I work for a company that cleans houses and offices. I can recommend you.* So, I started a job cleaning houses, clinics, parking lots and offices.

This was a wonderful chance to build our lives again, and I was so grateful. Yet, it was not normal for me to be normal. I was always worried that John was coming after us and would make me come back. Being outside anywhere with the kids felt weird because I was not used to the freedom of doing what I wanted to without someone watching or controlling me – and expecting his car to drive up at any moment. I had to get used to the way that most people, normal people, lived.

I worked at the cleaning job for almost a year, living at my stepsister's house, earning enough to pay the utilities and buy the things my kids needed. I often had to bring them with me to clean, and we all had fun working together and enjoying each other as we each did our chores, cleaning toilets, dusting, or taking out the trash. Little by little, I was bringing myself back to me, and I finally decided I was ready to go to the unemployment office for a better job.

It was my lucky day because the very day I went to the unemployment office and met with one of the staff people there to help me with my resume, she told me that FEMA (Federal Emergency Management Agency) was there hiring on the spot as part of a project to help the hurricane victims in a city near me. I got hired! It was a nice job, and $18 an hour was an enormous amount of money to me! However, the job was temporary, so after a few months, I was looking for work again.

More good fortune – the city really liked my performance and offered me a part-time position in the

Department of Parks and Recreation, serving senior citizens. Although I was happy to have this job and everyone was very kind, it was hard to provide for three kids on a part-time salary. I needed care for my toddler, Karla was in elementary school and Luis was now in middle school. And there was no financial support coming from John. So I was always searching for a better, full-time opportunity. Soon, I met somebody who worked for a college, and they hired me as an admissions representative. I loved the job, was able to buy a used car, the kids were doing well, and we were happy.

The impossible was becoming possible!

Chapter Twelve

Divorce: The Final Stand

In the months that followed, my little family got settled into our new life, my confidence and my bank account were building bit by bit, and a beautiful future lay before me. It was time to file for divorce, a process that ended up taking three years, mainly because John wouldn't sign the papers.

Over this time, John was still bothering me, calling me often to curse me and blame me for everything. Listening to his hurtful words and angry rants from a safe distance helped me get stronger and stronger in standing up for myself.

I would say to him, *Why are you calling me? You're not paying for my cell phone or my bills or to help the children. I don't need to hear you. It is what it is. Do not put it on me. I didn't go and abuse you. I didn't beat you up. I didn't put a pillow over your face until you couldn't breathe or put a gun to your head or abandon you when you just had a baby. I did not do these things. There's no need for me to speak to you. Please do not call me.*

Soon, I gave up trying to talk to him, and just sent his calls to voicemail and never listened to those messages.

As much as I could, I avoided any contact with him because I only heard lies after lies.

My resolve was so strong that I finally got him to sign the papers by "tricking" him into coming to a room at the courthouse where he found me sitting with two deputies by my side to make him take the action to sign. They then escorted me to my car because John was so outraged they feared for my safety. The divorce was final. I received no child support – which was fine with me because I wanted him out of my life. But he was given the right of visitation with his kids.

When I heard this, I was filled with dread. How was I going to do this without him finding me or having to see him again? But I had no choice.

We made the arrangements for my kids to go with their father for a visit over the weekend. I drove all around before going to his place to make sure he would not follow me and find out where we were living. As I drove up with the kids, I was nervous, but I was able to keep my fears hidden. I would never show any sign that I was afraid of him. Even though the familiar stomachache started up, I held Luis' hand tightly and rang the doorbell.

I saw pain in John's eyes, but it was far too late; I did not care anymore. It was my time to stand up for me and the kids. It was up to him to deal with the consequences of what he had done.

As he drove off with my precious babies, I felt such dread that I could barely concentrate on my drive home. He wouldn't tell me where they were going for the weekend, so I just sat in the living room for two hours, worried and unable to do anything, until I thought enough time had passed to call my daughter's phone to check on them. I had barely said hello to her when John grabbed her phone and said to me in a voice that chilled me to my bones, *I'm not bringing the kids back to you. You're never gonna see them again.*

I screamed, *Noooooooooooooo! Please, please don't do this!!* He wasn't listening, just going on and on, *I'm going to make sure they won't remember you no more! These are MY kids, and you won't see them ever again!*

He hung up, and I immediately called the police. When they came, I explained what he did, and the officer called John. They told him that for his own sake, he needed to understand that he had to return the children to their mother before Monday. If they were not back in school by Monday morning, he would be arrested. They cautioned him, *Don't worry, we WILL find you, so just remember that the kids need to be in class on time on Monday.*

That was the longest two days of my life. I had no idea if he would comply with the police and bring them back or not. I only had my faith. I was so joyful when I heard my phone ring on Sunday afternoon and it was him, ready to make arrangements to meet to return my children to me. Once again, he said he was sorry, and once again, his apologies meant nothing to me because I couldn't believe him.

Of course, I was reluctant for him to ever see my kids again, but visitation was court-ordered, so we were able to arrange for him to see them for a few hours only over scheduled periods of time. And that's what he did for a while.

Perhaps the divorce had shown him that I was strong and had no intentions of ever going back to him. Maybe – and I hoped this for all our sakes – he had found another woman he could care for and treat kindly. Whatever it was, he gradually stopped calling, and swearing at me or putting me down when he saw me. He started to live his life and move forward without me. And my children and I were able to move forward without him.

As for me, I was rediscovering myself – the Ana I had lost long ago and also the Ana I had now become, resourceful and strong with a beautiful family to love and a new commitment to living my very best life.

During those three years, I had been hesitant to accept invitations from my friends from church, coworkers or family to go anywhere because I was afraid he would find me. As I saw that he was beginning to go forward with his life, I began to get back my own life.

One day, my friend convinced me to take the kids to the park with her and her kids. As we sat on the bench watching our kids running and laughing freely, I looked at my beautiful children with something like surprise. They looked so free and happy. Nobody was controlling them. What a wonderful and amazing way to be! In that moment, I began to actually believe, *Hey, I get to be me! I get to smile! I get to choose! I get to jump into whatever I want to do!*

It was my moment of deliverance, and I never looked back.

Conclusion

I have forgiven my ex-husband because I know that I must, for myself and for my sanity in order to move forward. I have nothing against him, and for his own sake, I hope he has changed. I'm so happy that I was able to escape from him and build a life full of love, meaning and purpose. I have found love in my life from someone who cares for me just as I am, who treats me with kindness and respect. I am happy and content with my life with him, not because he "makes" me happy, but because *I choose* to stay happy!

Life is not always easy, but I believe deeply that if your path is difficult, it is because your purpose is bigger than you ever thought. My path has shown me what my purpose is – to help others learn from my experience so they can escape abuse themselves.

I now work as an associate director of financial aid for the local college, helping support my family and serve others. For years, I have worked with nurses, paramedics and EMTs to help train them in their important life-saving work.

I've become a professional speaker against domestic violence, in English and in Spanish. Recently, the Peloton Company (https://www.onepeloton.com/

company) invited me to perform a global video in Spanish to train their employees by sharing a portion of my narrative about domestic violence to help women like me. I've also given talks in local churches and other venues. My sincere hope is that this book will spread my story to even more people so they can be helped as well.

I'm overjoyed to know that I am able to use my experience to assist others. I am grateful for the purpose and meaning this work has brought to me and to my family. I thank God because otherwise, I would not have known how to protect myself and my children from my abuser. I have learned that:

- You are here to be loved, not to be exploited or harmed.

- You must believe in yourself.

- You must ask for help.

- You must talk to a friend or family member.

- And you must not make the same mistake that I made for so long –keeping silent.

It's time to speak up! You need to know that there are a lot of resources available (please look at the resources and guidance I shared at the end of this book). All you need is a strategy and the confidence to act. This is my message:

I am more than my trauma.

I am more than my abuse.

I am more than my scars.

I am what a survivor looks like.

I am Ana; I am a survivor of domestic violence.

And so are you. I stand with you.

"You are braver than you believe, stronger than you seem, and smarter than you think. But the most important thing is, even if we're apart...I'll always be with you."

— A.A. Milne, <u>Winnie the Pooh Library</u>

References and Resources

National Domestic Violence Hotline: Call 1.800.799.7233 (SAFE) or text "START" to 88788

Hours: 24/7. Languages: English, Spanish and 200+ through interpretation service

Helpful websites:

- National Domestic Violence Website: https://www.thehotline.org/

- Office on Women's Health/resources by state on violence against women: https://www.womenshealth.gov/relationships-and-safety/get-help/state-resources

- National Resource Center on Domestic Violence: https://www.nrcdv.org/

- Center for Disease Control and Prevention/ Violence prevention: https://www.cdc.gov/violenceprevention/intimatepartnerviolence/fastfact.html

- Moneygeek/financial support for women experiencing domestic violence: https://

**www.moneygeek.com/financial-planning/
resources/financial-help-women-abu-
sive-relationships/**

Important Messages to Share with the World about Domestic Violence

These are some of the messages I share with audiences when I am speaking. I share them with you here to help you if you are in a situation of abuse, or if you suspect a loved one is being mistreated:

"The abuser uses a false image to hide significant parts of their character."

"We should not be afraid to return home because we don't know what mood they'll be in."

"Always remember, I will either find a way to escape or I will make one."

"Just because my life LOOKED like a dream with my partner from the outside doesn't mean it wasn't a nightmare from the inside."

"And when you get to where you are going, turn around and help her too. For there was a time not long ago when she was you."

Important Information from the <u>National Resource Center on Domestic Violence (https:// www.thehotline.org/)</u>:

Remember: No one deserves to experience abuse of any kind - for any reason. And every type of abuse is serious. Recognizing abuse is the first step. Go to the website listed above to learn:

- The common signs of abusive behavior in a partner

- How to prepare to leave (you must have a plan or you will always go back)

- How to find support

- Always to trust your gut/intuition

About the Author

 Ana Williams has broken her silence to tell the story of her own experience of domestic violence so that other women may be inspired and supported to break free of their victimhood, as she has done. Ana is a professional speaker against domestic violence, in English and Spanish, for large audiences and small groups. She was invited by the Peloton Company to share her narrative in Spanish for a training video on domestic violence for their global employees. Ana has pledged to make meaning out of her own tragic experience by helping women find the resources, support and courage to leave their abusive situations forever for a fresh start. Ana Williams is also the Founder/Owner of AMA Legacy LLC.

Email: amamylegacy@gmail.com

Website: https://amalegacy.org/

Facebook: https://www.facebook.com/profile.php?id=100084878021366

TikTok: @anawilliams50

Instagram: https://www.instagram.com/imanaandim breakingthesilence/

Reviews

"I am Ana and I am Breaking the Silence" is full of power and punch about the story of a woman's survival and victory over domestic violence. *The portrayal of the abuser, their mindset, and obsession for control is gripping and brings the reader into the dark and frightening realm of abuse. Every mother should give her daughter a copy of this book before she begins to date. Bravo, Ana Williams, for sharing your courage and vulnerability so other women can be warned and supported. Great book.*
-Maureen Ryan Blake, Maureen Ryan Blake Media Production

"I am Ana" is a powerful, personal story of domestic violence which circulates the world. As you read Ana's thoughts, hear her fears, embrace her pain, the reader becomes one with her journey, and Ana's struggles merge into the heart of the reader page by page. Whether one may identify themselves or know the pain women suffer through this spoken of or silent journey, you wish for freedom, and peace for all women, children, or men that suffer through the hands and mind control of others. As Ana shares her detailed abusive experience with resources in which to go for help, she shows how

a little hope, faith, prayer, courage and support from others changed her life. Ana was once a silent sufferer of domestic violence, to become an author, advocate, and speaker for abusive domestic violence. It is a privilege to know Ana personally, her story, her success, and her willingness to help others. I smile with pride as it takes just one to let someone else know your story, then she lights her candle, breaks her silence, and "I am Ana" emerges. A must-read as your life or someone you love can also change.

-Toni Stone Bruce, Author, Motivational Speaker, Coach
Founder/CEO Precious Stones 4 Life, LLC

Ana's book is such a powerful story of a woman who is a survivor of domestic abuse. She highlights many telltale characteristics of her abuser to communicate the specific patterns of abuse she endured during her harrowing experience with her ex-husband. God set her free and she is now on a new journey to help others in a similar situation. This book is a powerful tool in the battle against domestic violence.

-MacKenzie Nelson, Best-Selling International Author, "My Father's Feathers"